DEBORAH BRUCE

Deborah Bruce has been a theatre director for twenty years
and has now started writing. Her other plays include
The Distance, which was a finalist in the 2013 Susan Smith
Blackburn Prize, *Godchild* at the Hampstead Theatre, and *Same*
for the National Theatre Connections Festival 2014.

Other Titles in this Series

Deborah Bruce

SAME

NICK HERN BOOKS
London
www.nickhernbooks.co.uk

A Nick Hern Book

Same first published in Great Britain in 2014 as a single edition paperback by
Nick Hern Books Limited, The Glasshouse, 49a Goldhawk Road, London W12 8QP

Same copyright © 2014 Deborah Bruce

Deborah Bruce has asserted her moral right to be identified as the author of this
work

Cover image by Joanne Preston, a member of DramaLab Jersey, for the
company's production of *Same*, performed at the Jersey Opera House, Bristol Old
Vic and the National Theatre, London, as part of NT Connections 2014.

Designed and typeset by Nick Hern Books, London
Printed in Great Britain by Mimeo Ltd, Cambridgeshire PE29 6XX

A CIP catalogue record for this book is available from the British Library

ISBN 978 1 84842 408 1

MIX
Paper from
responsible sources
FSC® C019549

Same was commissioned as part of the 2014 National Theatre Connections Festival and premiered by youth theatres across the UK, including a performance at the National Theatre in July 2014.

Each year the National Theatre asks ten writers to create new plays to be performed by young theatre companies all over the country. From Scotland to Cornwall and Northern Ireland to Norfolk, Connections celebrates great new writing for the stage – and the energy, commitment and talent of young theatremakers.

www.nationaltheatre.org.uk/connections

For my grandmothers,
Pru Bruce and Paula Barnett,
and their great-grandchildren,
Barney and Nell Herrin

Characters

EMMA, *sixteen*
FAY, *Emma's sister, fifteen*
YOUNG HARRY, *Emma's brother, thirteen*
SARAH, *Emma's cousin, fourteen*
CALLUM, *Sarah's brother, twelve*
JO-JO, *Emma's cousin, thirteen*

CLARE, *late seventies*
MARION, *Clare's sister, eighty*
SADIE, *late seventies*
ALF, *eighties*
EDDIE *eighties*
GRACE, *seventies*

JOSIE
HARRY

Note on the Text

The action takes place in an old people's home in a small town.

Depending on the number of actors, there can be doubling between the young and old characters. Or not.

The older characters were originally written to be played by teenagers with the intention that it enables the audience to see the young person inside the old. I strongly encourage actors and directors to steer well clear of any 'old person' acting.

A forward slash (/) in the middle of a line denotes an overlap in dialogue, so that the next person to speak starts speaking before the first person has finished speaking.

Scene One

A bedroom in an old people's home. Half-packed up. Boxes on the floor, some of the pictures taken down and leaning against the wall. No sheets on the bed.

There are six teenagers in the room.

EMMA, FAY *and* YOUNG HARRY *sit on the bed.* SARAH *stands by the door.* CALLUM *sits on the floor playing on a Nintendo DS, and* JO-JO *sits on a stool at a dressing table.*

They are all looking at screens except YOUNG HARRY.

Silence.

FAY. Aaw, thanks for liking my picture, Jo-Jo.

JO-JO. You're welcome. Thank you for liking mine.

EMMA. Have you changed your profile picture?

JO-JO. No –

FAY. Is it that one with your hair tonged?

JO-JO. The one with my friend's puppy.

FAY / EMMA. Aaaaw –

FAY. Oh my God, that was so sweet.

YOUNG HARRY. Get off Facebook.

FAY. Sarah. Are you logged in?

SARAH. I'm talking to my friend.

FAY. On Facebook?

SARAH. On WhatsApp.

FAY. I've just sent you a message on Facebook.

SARAH. Saying what?

FAY. Go on it.

SARAH. Okay.

Pause.

Aaaw. Sweet.

EMMA. What is it?

YOUNG HARRY. What'd'you send her a message for? She's right there.

SARAH. I've liked it.

EMMA. Let's see.

FAY *shows her her phone screen.*

YOUNG HARRY. Get off fucking Facebook.

EMMA *slaps* YOUNG HARRY *round the head.*

EMMA. Oh my God, I cannot believe you just swore in Nan's room. Oh my God, Harry, I am not joking.

YOUNG HARRY. So? She can't hear me, can she?

FAY. Harry!

EMMA. Oh my God, Harry, you are so disrespectful.

YOUNG HARRY. What?

EMMA. Sorry, Sarah. Sorry, Callum.

FAY. Oh my God, I am so embarrassed for you.

YOUNG HARRY. What?

FAY. Sorry, everyone, for my disrespectful brother.

EMMA *looks up and puts her hand on her heart.*

EMMA. Sorry, Nanna.

FAY (*looks up too, puts her hand on her heart too*). Yeah, sorry, Nanna.

Silence.

YOUNG HARRY. What though? She can't hear me, can she?

No one says anything. FAY *and* EMMA *give him a look.*

Well, she can't, can she?

FAY *glares at him.*

You're all on Facebook. That's not very respectful, is it?

FAY. I'm putting that Nan's died actually. I'm writing a whole thing about her thank you very much.

YOUNG HARRY. Putting it all over Facebook, what's respectful about that?

Pause.

She wasn't even on Facebook.

EMMA. Shut up or I'm going to tell Mum that you said the f-word in Nan's room.

FAY. Just because you've had your phone confiscated. You wouldn't even be speaking to us now if you had your phone. God!

Silence.

SARAH. Aaah, that's so sweet, Fay.

FAY. Thanks.

SARAH. Shall I like it?

FAY. How many likes has it got? –

YOUNG HARRY. 'How many likes has it got?' –

SARAH. Three. –

YOUNG HARRY. Who cares? –

JO-JO. Don't like it. It's like you're liking that Nan's died. –

FAY. Who's liked it?

SARAH. Oh yeah! Oh, I pressed it, just as you said that! I've liked it!

JO-JO. Unlike it! Press unlike!

SARAH. There's no unlike!

EMMA. Press like again. It unlikes it.

SARAH. Oh my God! I can't believe I liked it! Oh, I hope she doesn't. What if she? Sorry, Nanna! Oh no!

SARAH *starts to cry.*

EMMA *goes to her.*

EMMA. Oh no, don't. Come on. Harry, get up and let Sarah sit on the bed.

YOUNG HARRY *gets up.*

Come on, sit with me and Fay. Do you want Harry to go and get your dad?

SARAH. No, it's okay.

EMMA. It's okay to cry, we've all been crying.

JO-JO. Nan would have wanted us to cry. That sounds weird, but do you know what I mean?

FAY. I know what you mean –

JO-JO. She would have been like, 'Let it all out, come on, have a hanky.'

YOUNG HARRY. Shall I go and get Uncle Andrew?

FAY. She said no.

JO-JO. She'd have been like, 'Better out than in.'

YOUNG HARRY. That's for if you belched –

SARAH. I just feel so bad, I hadn't seen her since Easter. You all saw her all the time, me and Callum didn't.

YOUNG HARRY *belches.*

FAY. Oh My God, Harry, what are you doing? / Fay's *crying.*

EMMA. Well, you see your other nan, don't you, like loads and stuff.

FAY (*to* YOUNG HARRY). What are you *like*?

YOUNG HARRY. I can't help it, can I?

FAY (*to* YOUNG HARRY). Yes you *can*.

SARAH. I know. But, I really miss seeing her, and now, I can't. Do you know what I mean?

EMMA. I know.

FAY. I know.

YOUNG HARRY. Shall I go and get Uncle Andrew?

EMMA. Be quiet.

SARAH. And I'm not being funny, I know she loved us all the same and all of that.

YOUNG HARRY. I think she loved me just a little bit more than all of you, actually.

FAY. Oh my *God*, Harry, are you for actual real?

YOUNG HARRY. I'm joking! Gosh! Chill *out*.

SARAH. It's just, you lot all saw her loads before she died, and me and Callum, well, we didn't, kind of thing.

EMMA. She wasn't herself, Sarah, honestly, you are better off not having seen that.

FAY. She was like demented and stuff –

EMMA. Not demented –

YOUNG HARRY. I was going to say! Bit rude.

EMMA. Yeah, she had dementia, obviously, so she got confused about who people were, sometimes.

JO-JO. Saying strange things, things that didn't make like total sense.

YOUNG HARRY. It's not like she was frothing at the mouth.

FAY. Oh my *God*, why don't you like – (*Mouths.*) *fuck off*.

SARAH. Did she know who Mel and Alison were?

YOUNG HARRY. I am going to text Mum and tell her that you said fuck off.

FAY. Yeah? Really? You haven't got your phone, so good luck with that.

YOUNG HARRY. Jo-Jo, can I borrow your phone please?

JO-JO. No.

EMMA. She kind of did know Mum, mostly.

FAY. Yeah, she knew Mum, and she knew Auntie Alison, and she knew us, didn't she?

YOUNG HARRY. Sarah, can I borrow your phone please?

SARAH. I bet she wouldn't have known me and Callum, she hadn't seen us since Easter. / I hate my dad.

EMMA. Of course she would have known you, oh my *God*.

FAY. Oh my God, Sarah, she *so* would have known you, wouldn't she, Emma?

EMMA. Of course.

SARAH. Why didn't my dad bring us over here? I hate him.

Pause.

EMMA. Are you all right, Callum?

CALLUM. Yeah.

EMMA. What are you playing?

CALLUM. Super Mario.

EMMA. That's good.

The girls all sit on the bed.

Are you all right, Sarah?

SARAH. I can't believe I liked that post.

FAY. It wasn't that you liked that she was dead, though, it wasn't like that.

SARAH. I know. I just wanted to. Support the sentiment.

FAY. Yes.

SARAH. I just wanted to be part of it.

EMMA. Oh my God, you are.

Pause. EMMA, FAY *and* JO-JO *all look at each other.*

SARAH. What was it like when you last saw her? Did she know you were there?

JO-JO. Kind of.

EMMA. Not really.

JO-JO. Yeah, not really.

EMMA. She was very confused the last time.

SARAH. What did she say to you?

EMMA. Nothing really, I can't remember exactly.

JO-JO. No, I can't remember exactly.

YOUNG HARRY. You weren't there.

JO-JO. I was.

YOUNG HARRY. It was just me and Emma and Fay the last time, you were at a sleepover.

JO-JO. I *was* there, I was there the last time we saw her.

YOUNG HARRY. You were probably there the last time *you* saw her, but you weren't there the last time *we* saw her, when she was going on about Granddad and asking for Uncle Andrew.

EMMA. Harry.

YOUNG HARRY. What? I'm just saying.

SARAH. Did Nanna ask for my dad?

EMMA. Sort of but she wasn't awake. She hadn't been properly awake for two days.

SARAH. What did she say?

EMMA. Just like, 'Is Andrew here? Where's Andrew?' That kind of thing. But like talking in her sleep.

FAY. 'I want Andrew', she said that as well.

SARAH. Oh my God.

EMMA. But she knew that he was like really busy with work and stuff, she knew that he would come when he could.

SARAH. Oh my God.

EMMA. It's all right. Honestly, Sarah, I can't explain, it wasn't like being with Nanna. We were there and stuff but she wasn't like there, it was like she was in a really deep sleep.

Your dad saw her loads before she was ill. That's the main thing.

SARAH. Shit.

Pause.

FAY. Oh my God! I can't believe it's got, like, thirteen likes. I only posted it, like, ten minutes ago. I'm so popular! Jokes.

YOUNG HARRY. Yeah you're so popular, everyone's really happy your nan's dead.

FAY. I wish you were dead.

JO-JO. Oh my God, I can't believe you said that!

EMMA. You don't understand, Jo-Jo, because you're an only child.

SARAH. I don't know what's going on, I'm all over the place.

EMMA. Everyone is. Mum locked her car keys in the car before we drove over this morning. Then she banged her knee on the table in the hall and started crying. / She's a nervous wreck.

YOUNG HARRY. That was funny.

FAY. You're a tosser.

YOUNG HARRY. Dad laughed.

FAY. Dad wasn't even there so that just shows what a liar you are. Why don't you shut up if you haven't got anything useful to say. Go and sit in the TV room, that Barbara woman said we could.

YOUNG HARRY. I'm not going in there, have you seen them? It's like *Shaun of the Dead*.

EMMA. You are so disrespectful.

YOUNG HARRY. They're all dribbling and shitting themselves.

JO-JO. Who's Rachel Charlie?

FAY. A girl in my year. Why?

JO-JO. She's liked your post about Nanny.

FAY. Oh my God, what's she liking my post for? She's such an idiot. She was the one who said about America –

EMMA. Oh my God, you have to tell them that, that was so funny –

FAY. She was like, 'Ya, I've been to three places in America, New York, LA and Paris.' We were like, 'Uh?' Oh my God, so funny.

JO-JO. Paris isn't in America.

YOUNG HARRY. We're in the company of a genius –

FAY. I know, that's like the whole point. Aaw, Jo-Jo, you're so sweet.

Pause.

SARAH. I feel so bad.

EMMA. Why didn't your dad bring you over, do you think?

SARAH. He's gone weird.

JO-JO. Didn't he want to come and see Nanna?

SARAH. I don't know. Everything's gone weird.

CALLUM *looks at her.*

Mum's sort of, in a relationship.

Beat.

EMMA. Seriously?

FAY. What with like a boyfriend?

YOUNG HARRY. No, with like a unicorn –

EMMA. Oh my God, Sarah, seriously?

CALLUM. What do you have to tell them that for?

SARAH. Of course I'm going to tell them, they're our family.

FAY. Oh my God, I can't believe your mum's got a boyfriend.

CALLUM. Just shut up about it.

JO-JO. Does he live at your house?

SARAH. No, he's got his own house, near the retail park.

FAY. Does he like stay over and stuff?

CALLUM. What are you telling them for?

FAY. Has he got his stuff at your house?

SARAH. I can tell them what I like.

CALLUM. No you can't.

SARAH. Yes I can. He's called David, he's a history teacher.

FAY. Oh. My. God.

SARAH. Not like in a school, like in a university-type thing, like a college.

FAY. I was going to say, what if he was like your history teacher –

SARAH. He's got dyed hair.

FAY. Oh my God, fail. / Epic fail.

EMMA. Is he nice though?

YOUNG HARRY. He *dyes* his hair.

SARAH. He's all right. He wears Converse and stuff.

CALLUM. Stop talking about it.

SARAH. Why?

CALLUM. Because.

Pause.

Nan's dead.

Silence.

JO-JO. There's a packet of Wine Gums in this drawer.

YOUNG HARRY. Awkward. Change the subject.

JO-JO. Shall I open them?

EMMA. Your mum said not to touch anything, so / don't look in the drawers, Jo-Jo.

YOUNG HARRY. Not Wine Gums, she was talking about like letters and stuff. Not like Wine Gums and shit. / Give us one.

FAY. Stop swearing!

YOUNG HARRY. She'll of bought them for us anyway. They'll be for us. She'd of wanted us to eat them.

EMMA. Auntie Alison said leave everything as it is, they haven't done the inventory. They have to go through everything with the manager. Then we can have stuff.

YOUNG HARRY. Not Wine Gums!

FAY. They haven't done the inventory.

YOUNG HARRY. You don't put bloody Wine Gums on an inventory. / She means like jewellery, valuable stuff.

FAY. Harry!

JO-JO. Oh my God, did you hear, my mum had to get Nan's wedding rings off?

YOUNG HARRY. One packet of Wine Gums, unopened. Check.

EMMA. I know.

SARAH. When?

JO-JO. After it happened. She had to twist them off, she had to get hand cream and rub it in, to make it slippery. They wouldn't come off.

FAY. Oh my God, that's so sad.

YOUNG HARRY. One screwed-up tissue and half a packet of Polos. Check.

EMMA. She never took her wedding ring off. She never took her engagement ring off even when she went into hospital. They said she had to and she refused. She said they'd have to cut her finger off.

SARAH. Oh my God. So did your mum have to rub the cream in?

JO-JO. Yeah. She had to twist them. She had to pull really hard. She said Auntie Mel said maybe they should leave them on. They felt bad. They would have left them on if she was going to be buried, my mum said. It seemed a waste just to burn them.

YOUNG HARRY. Hey! That's sick.

FAY. Shut up.

YOUNG HARRY. If I'd said that you'd have done your nut.

FAY. Yeah because you're an idiot and you'd have just said it to shock everyone and to show off.

YOUNG HARRY. No I wouldn't –

FAY. Jo-Jo's actually telling us something, we are having A Conversation.

CALLUM. Isn't Nan going to be buried?

JO-JO. She's being cremated.

CALLUM. Why isn't she going to be buried?

JO-JO. Because she's being cremated. Cremation's more environmentally friendly.

CALLUM. She has to be buried. She wanted to be buried.

YOUNG HARRY. Nan didn't do recycling. She covered her recycling-crate thing in wrapping paper and put her Christmas tree on it.

CALLUM. Who said she was going to be cremated?

YOUNG HARRY. Nan wouldn't be bothered about being recycled.

EMMA. Your dad was on about the crematorium to Mum.

CALLUM. What does he know about it? He's a dickhead.

Pause.

YOUNG HARRY. How come he's allowed to say that?

FAY. Because Uncle Andrew and Helen have split up and he's upset.

YOUNG HARRY. Yeah, what if I'm upset as well.

FAY. Aaaw, diddums. What about?

YOUNG HARRY. Nan. Obviously.

FAY. We all are. Obviously.

Pause.

EMMA. Okay, let's all go round and say something we remember about Nan.

YOUNG HARRY. Everything, obviously. She only died on Thursday.

FAY. She doesn't *mean* it like that.

EMMA. I mean, the real Nanna, before she got dementia, the Nanna *before*.

JO-JO. 'Go and sit in the sunshine and untangle your knickers.'

SARAH. 'If you can't say something nice.'

EMMA. Wait, let's all go round one by one. Let's do it properly. Harry, get in the circle. Callum, put your DS down for a minute. Let's all do it together.

FAY. The cousins!

EMMA. Aaaw.

JO-JO. The Wombles, like Granddad called us.

SARAH. Oh my God, yes! And things about Granddad as well.

(*Starts to cry.*) I can't believe they've both gone!

JO-JO. Granddad used to dance like he was walking but standing still.

SARAH. He called me his little princess –

JO-JO. And me! –

YOUNG HARRY. And me!

FAY. Shut *up*, Harry.

YOUNG HARRY. Oh no, hang on, he called me his little soldier –

FAY. Oh my God, that is so sexist! Sorry, Granddad, but oh my God –

EMMA. He used to say to Nanna, 'Oh, Josie, do you remember when I could climb a ladder? Do you remember when I could run round to the shop and back in a commercial break?'

FAY. 'Do you remember when I – ?' All the time, he used to say that!

EMMA. Say stuff about Nanna as well –

SARAH. 'Oh, well, we'll never run out!'

FAY. Oh my God, all the tins and tea bags in the garage. Oh, I miss that house so much. Do you remember? –

YOUNG HARRY. No, I've got Alzheimer's –

FAY. Shut up, you're not funny, why do you spoil everything?

CALLUM. The toilet was in the garden.

SARAH. Not the only toilet, there were two in the house –

CALLUM. It had mould in it –

FAY. There were flower fairies in the shed, they left sweets for us –

YOUNG HARRY. That was Nanna –

FAY. Durr, I *know*.

> JO-JO *sings the opening line of 'My Girl Josephine' by Fats Domino.*

> JO-JO, EMMA, SARAH *and* FAY *sing the next few lines together, until –*

JO-JO (*forgetting the lyric, singing*). Something about an umbrella, la la la la la.

> It was a crying shame, or something!

EMMA. Go on.

JO-JO. I don't remember the rest of it.

> FAY *remembers and sings the line about the umbrella correctly.*

> I can't remember the words.

FAY. Try. You do.

JO-JO. I'll google the lyrics.

> *They sit in silence for a bit.*

SARAH. Nanna and Granddad had such a perfect marriage, didn't they. I feel bad for them that their children didn't, you know, follow in their footsteps.

YOUNG HARRY. Our mum and dad are still together –

SARAH. Yeah, apart from them –

EMMA. Only just –

YOUNG HARRY. What do you mean?

FAY. Don't say that. / They're fine.

YOUNG HARRY. What do you mean 'only just'?

EMMA. Nothing, they're fine.

SARAH. I just meant our parents. And Auntie Alison and your dad.

JO-JO. Nanna said it wasn't Mum's fault.

SARAH. I'm not saying it's anyone's fault.

CALLUM. Shut up about it then.

YOUNG HARRY. Why did you say 'only just', are Mum and Dad going to split up?

FAY. I know what you mean, marriage is different now, it doesn't mean what it used to mean in Nanny and Granddad's day, does it? They didn't have like loads of ways of finding out about each other before marriage, like Facebook and checking out people's profiles and looking at photos of their ex-girlfriends and stuff. They just had to get on with it. They had to get to know each other on their own and work things out on their own.

YOUNG HARRY. Are Mum and Dad going to split up?

EMMA / FAY. No! Shut up.

SARAH. They couldn't like text each other to say sorry if one of them stropped off, they had to work much harder, I think, I think their relationships were much stronger, do you?

FAY. Yeah, I think their generation were more respectful to each other, I think they took the wedding vows much more seriously, because they'd had to work so hard already, and like getting divorced was really bad.

JO-JO. For richer for poorer, till death do us part, for as long as us both shall live, and stuff.

FAY. People make up our own vows now, they're obviously not going to be as good.

EMMA. They are, it's better not to have to say all that stuff, I think, it's better to be more realistic, more specific about what you want your relationship to be like.

YOUNG HARRY. What's the point of getting married anyway if you can just get a divorce?

FAY. Shut up, we're not talking about that.

YOUNG HARRY. You can get a 'Happy Divorce' cake in Tesco, it says like 'Happy Divorce', and there's like a groom falling off a building –

EMMA. It's a pedestal.

YOUNG HARRY. And he's cracked his head open and there's like blood everywhere –

EMMA. There's not –

FAY. Shut up, you can't get a cake of it –

EMMA. You can. / There isn't blood though.

YOUNG HARRY. You can.

SARAH. I bet Nanna and Granddad were disappointed when Dad left Mum. I bet they thought he hadn't worked hard enough at their relationship.

JO-JO. My mum worked really hard at her relationship with my dad but he moved to Totnes so there wasn't really any point.

SARAH. Mum said Granddad drove all the way to where Dad was staying with his friend, to try and get him to change his mind but he pretended not to be in and Granddad had to come all the way back in the rush hour. Mum said Granddad was really angry and banged his fist and broke the little window in the washroom. There's still a crack in it.

I can't believe Dad didn't come and see Nanna. I can't believe he left it too late.

FAY. Let's remember nice things.

JO-JO. Let's talk about Christmas.

YOUNG HARRY. Let's talk about fluffy bunnies and hair clips.

FAY. Shut up, you moron –

EMMA. Do you remember when Nanna went to bed on
    Christmas Day when she was ill and she said, 'I don't want
    to hear any one of you trying to be quiet.' Oh, lovely Nanny.

SARAH. Were we there that Christmas?

EMMA. No, I don't think you were.

FAY. I remember playing Solitaire on the patio, and going to the
    bring-and-buy sales at the church –

JO-JO. Choc-ices –

EMMA. 'I hope you've got your vest on' –

FAY. When we all danced to *The Muppets* with the mop.

EMMA. When Harry was born and Nanna said he looked like
    Granddad and Granddad said 'poor sod', and then Mum
    called him Harry and Nanna cried.

SARAH. I wish she was here.

EMMA. She is in a way, she's in all of us.

JO-JO. I've got her name.

SARAH. You're so lucky.

    JO-JO *comes over to* FAY *and* EMMA *with her phone and
    shows them the screen.*

    FAY *and* EMMA *sing the first few lines of 'My Girl
    Josephine' by Fats Domino.*

    Pause.

    Who sings that?

EMMA. Fats Domino.

    JO-JO *sings the next line.*

FAY. Fats?

    SARAH *and* JO-JO *sing the next line together.*

    You can't call him Fats.

EMMA. That's his name.

FAY. What? His parents called him Fats?

EMMA. Not his parents / probably.

FAY. Oh my God, that's so un-PC.

EMMA. It's like a nickname –

FAY. Was he fat?

EMMA. I don't know what he looked like, Nanny played the record, do you remember a picture on the cover, Jo-Jo?

JO-JO. No. He sounds, a bit fat. I'll google images.

FAY. Sorry, but that is so wrong, that is so bad for his self-esteem, he could have been so damaged by that, God!

Pause.

CALLUM. I remember when I was sick off school one day just before Mum and Dad split up and Dad was supposed to be looking after me but he couldn't so he drove me to Nanny's house and I was watching a *Simpsons* DVD.

YOUNG HARRY. Was it *Simpsons the Movie*?

CALLUM. No, just the series.

YOUNG HARRY. That's mine.

CALLUM. And Dad and Nan went into the garage –

YOUNG HARRY. But you can watch it.

CALLUM. And they had a massive row.

SARAH. No, Callum.

CALLUM. And I could hear them while I was watching the DVD. And Dad said fuck, and Nanny said she was glad he wasn't her real son, and then she cried and said she was sorry and Dad drove off without saying goodbye to me, and she was saying that she would never forgive herself and that she would take her sorryness to her grave with her.

SARAH. What did you have to tell them that for?

CALLUM. I'm just saying. That's how I know she definitely wanted to be buried.

Blackout.

Scene Two

A large sitting room in an old people's home, with high-backed chairs in almost a semicircle.

CLARE, SADIE, ALF, GRACE *and* EDDIE *sit in the chairs.*

MARION *stands with her coat on, beside* CLARE's *chair.*

MARION. Well, I didn't know. No one said.

CLARE. It was last-minute. They didn't tell us it was going to be held here till this morning.

MARION. I called to say I was coming as normal. I always come on a Wednesday. No one said not to.

CLARE. Who did you speak to?

MARION. I don't know. Not Barbara.

CLARE. Wasn't it Barbara?

MARION. No, it wasn't Barbara. Barbara would've said.

SADIE. It could have been Sally.

CLARE. Sally, that's right. It would have been her. Now, you see she's new, she might not have thought to say.

MARION. She should have said.

CLARE. She's new.

MARION. I wouldn't have come. Or at least I could have come later. Or earlier. I could have come yesterday. Well, not yesterday because I had pilates, but I could have come Monday. After Spanish.

CLARE. Well, you're here now, eh?

MARION. All the black cars outside. It's very morbid.

CLARE. Well. You're here now.

Silence.

MARION. So is no one allowed in the dining room then?

CLARE. It's for the funeral guests. They have their tea in there. Only half an hour or so. You can go in if you want to go to the funeral. Everyone's welcome, Barbara said.

ALF. I'm not going in there.

CLARE. Do you want to go in there?

MARION. Whose is it?

ALF. I'm not going in there.

CLARE. Josie Fowler. Lung cancer and dementia. Room Four next to the airing cupboard. I only saw her once in the whole time she was here so I'm not going in.

ALF. Death tramping through the lounge, they should hold the funeral at the house.

SADIE. They sold her house to pay for the home.

ALF. What about the daughter's house? What about the son? Haven't they got a house? What do we want reminding of dying in here? We can't forget it long enough to need reminding of it. Piling the wreaths up in the hall. 'Do you want some flowers in your room, Mr Barratt?' No thank you very much, I know where they've come from and I know where you can stick them.

Laughter.

SADIE. Those lilies get their pollen all over your sleeve every time you brush past, they're a terror.

Pause.

MARION. Well, I'm going to see if I can get a chair from somewhere. Anybody need anything while I'm going walkabouts?

SADIE / CLARE. No.

MARION exits.

ALF. You wouldn't catch me going in there, I tell you.

Pause.

I wouldn't go in there if you paid me.

Pause.

EDDIE. Because in its heyday of course, you know, there were twenty-five thousand dockers working on The Mersey. That's how it was. Up and down Great Homer Street, you'd get the

smells, the fresh food being cooked up, from the markets. And
we supported each other, the core of the society we were.
None of your scroungers, and your wasters, sitting around on
their backsides waiting to be given something for nothing. We
earned a good wage, we knew our manners, always well
turned out. I never heard my father swear, not once. Never
owed a penny to anyone in his life. Not like these days. Not
like the banks these days, messing it all up for everyone,
throwing money around then wanting it back bigger.

CLARE. She'll need to get a chair from the activities room, she
won't be able to lift the ones in the hall.

SADIE. What?

CLARE. She won't be able to lift the chairs in the hall. She'll
need to get a chair from the activities room, one of the
plastic ones.

SADIE. Who?

CLARE. My sister. My sister's gone to get a chair.

ALF. They better be quick about it, that's all I can say. Standing
round talking. Where were they when she was alive? Hadn't
got so much to say then, had they?

EDDIE. Langton, Brocklebank, Carrier, Canada, Huskisson,
Sandon, Sandon Half Tide, Wellington.

MARION *returns with a chair. She places it next to* CLARE.

CLARE. Did you get that from the activities room?

MARION. I don't know, a nice young man found it for me –

CLARE. He'll of got it from the activities room, didn't I say that?

SADIE. Yes.

EDDIE. Because most of them are filled in now, of course.

MARION. Pardon?

EDDIE. But in the forties, 1947, I started, yes, it was a going
concern then, well over three quarters of us were dailies,
mind, not until the strike, and they guaranteed our working
hours, didn't they, it was a good wage.

MARION. Oh, yes, well, that's good.

EDDIE. My father, honest to God, now, he never owed a penny to anyone in his life, not a penny. He was a gentleman. And his father, and *his* father. Settled in Scotland Road, he did, over from Ireland, eleven of them there were, 1845 it was. Worked on the docks since then we all have. Just four hundred of them now. That's it. Four hundred left out of twenty-five thousand. A hundred and fifty of them in the terminal. There's not the loyalty now, not the solidarity. There was Seaforth, Gladstone, Hornby, Alexandra, Langton, Brocklebank, it was next along.

MARION. Is that right, oh!

CLARE. I said to Sadie, I said, 'She'll have to get one from the activities room because she won't be able to lift one of the heavy ones from the hall.'

MARION. My arthritis, I can't lift the kettle some mornings.

CLARE. You should go back to Dr Monk, I'm sick of saying it.

MARION. Well, I will, when I get round to it. I've got too much on! I'm in and out of here every five minutes, aren't I? And that bus timetable's a fiction. Had to wait nearly three quarters of an hour when I left last week. The dogs were beside themselves when I eventually got home.

EDDIE. But God's watching over me, 'Eddie,' he said, 'Eddie, you listen to me. You have to let it go, nothing lasts for ever, you're an old man now, and those days have gone.' I can see it, clear as you like, from the north side to the south, sun coming up first thing, 'All right, Ed!' It went Huskisson, Sandon, Sandon Half Tide, Wellington, Bramley-Moore. 'All right, Ed!' 'All right, Robbie!' We looked out for each other, always watching my back, Robbie.

MARION. Oh, really? Well.

CLARE. You don't have to keep interacting with him, he doesn't need you to, he's happy enough talking to himself.

MARION. Oh. It seems a bit rude to ignore him.

CLARE. We all do, he doesn't mind.

MARION. Well, it'll be what he's used to, won't it, so understaffed they are in here. No time to turn round, most of them. Let alone talk to people.

CLARE. Sadie and I have put our names down for the memory-box project, haven't we, Sadie?

SADIE. Yes.

CLARE. So we've got that coming up.

MARION. That's nice.

CLARE. Yes. I might need some things bringing from home.

MARION. Like what? I've got that nightie, remind me to leave it at the desk before I go. It's a twelve, they didn't have a ten. You've lost so much weight.

CLARE. Can you bring my school reports, and some photographs from the purple album, just bring the album. And the key ring I bought in Tenerife, and the Spanish postcard with the Spanish dress stuck on that Mum and Auntie Phyllis sent us –

MARION. What? / Hang on.

CLARE. And Bruce Forsyth's autograph, it's in the wicker box on my windowsill –

MARION. What are you going to do with all that nonsense?

CLARE. Put it in my memory box. Me and Sadie have put our names down.

ALF. I'm not having anything to do with that bollocks. What do you need to put memories in a shitting box for? They're in your head, aren't they? That not a good enough box for you?

CLARE. I'm not talking to you, I'm having a private conversation with my visitor.

ALF. Nothing's private unless you're sitting with the deaf ones.

CLARE. So can you bring those things in, please, Marion? And a box.

MARION. What kind of box?

SADIE. I think they provide a box.

MARION. Well, I should think so, what kind of project is this, you have to provide all the materials yourself!

CLARE. It's a very prestigious organisation actually, they are a nationwide –

MARION. What do they actually do?

CLARE. They are a nationwide organisation. There were limited places.

MARION. I see. What's it *for*?

ALF. Nowt.

CLARE. It's for your self-esteem.

ALF. Ha! I've heard it all now!

CLARE. It's so you can assemble all your memories in one place –

ALF. They're in one place already! Your head!

CLARE. – and then you can decorate the box with personal things about your personality, newspaper cuttings and recipes, they said. And then you leave it outside your door so that any new members of the team, or if you need a nurse or anyone comes to interact with you, they can look in the box and learn all about you before they meet you.

Pause.

MARION. I see.

CLARE. What are you saying it like that for?

MARION. I'm not saying it like anything.

CLARE. So can you bring me the bits when you come next week?

MARION. Well, if I remember.

CLARE. Can't you write yourself a note or something?

MARION. Well, yes, I'll have to. I've got my watercolours class on Friday, and the fundraiser for Mozambique on the Monday. I've got a dental appointment on the Tuesday so –

CLARE. What's wrong?

MARION. Just the hygienist, but I'll need to remember that, so.

SADIE. You're keeping yourself busy, aren't you?

MARION. Yes I am. I'm going to nip this nightie over to the desk before I forget, actually. Just like me to end up taking it all the way back home again!

MARION *exits with the nightie.*

SADIE. She's keeping herself busy, isn't she, Clare?

CLARE. Yes.

Pause.

SADIE. My granddaughter's sending me my bits and pieces in a Jiffy Bag registered delivery. Barbara helped me send her an email about it.

CLARE. Oh well, that's good, isn't it?

SADIE. Yes it is.

Pause.

ALF. You'll be in a box soon enough I say, a bloody coffin! That's the only memory box I'll be doing. And no one'll be rifling through that before they meet me, thank you very much.

EDDIE. George's Basin, George's Dock, Manchester, Canning –

ALF. It's worse than the shitting *Shipping Forecast* sitting next to him –

EDDIE. Old Dock, Canning Half Tide, Albert. All the way down, mostly filled in now, of course. Twenty-five thousand dockers we were, never took a day off work sick, never owed a penny to anyone in his life, my father. Went to see Everton play every other weekend, like a religion it was, singing all the songs, talking about it all week, seeing us through.

MARION *re-enters, pushing* GRACE *in a wheelchair.*

MARION. Look who I found sitting all by herself in the hall. No one at the desk. No one anywhere. It's like the, umm, the umm –

ALF. They'll all be eating biscuits and talking shite, couldn't give a toss about us. We could all have had a stroke, they wouldn't care. Sitting here with blood trickling out our ears. 'Blah blah blah.'

MARION. It's like the, umm –

SADIE. Are you all right, Grace?

MARION. She's all right now, aren't you? You're all right now, you're back in the gang! All on your own out there! No one around. It's like the, you know.

SADIE. You okay, Grace?

She's very frail, she gets anxious easily.

MARION. There you are, okay now, aren't you?

GRACE. Is it nearly time?

MARION. Time for what, love?

GRACE. Are they here?

MARION. Who?

GRACE. The people for Harry's wife.

CLARE. Harry who?

GRACE. Harry Fowler. Are they here?

CLARE. I don't know what she means, I think you better get Barbara –

MARION. Do you want me to get Barbara, Grace? Do you need your inhaler?

GRACE. Who?

SADIE. Do you need someone to see to you? Shall I call?

MARION. I can go.

CLARE. You're supposed to be visiting me, not running around the place!

MARION. Well, I know!

CLARE. I was telling you about the memory project, wasn't I?

MARION. Shall I get you a cup of tea, Grace? / It's no trouble.

CLARE. I think it's a lovely thing to do. I've been really looking forward to it. Sadie and I were the first to put our names down, weren't we?

SADIE. Yes.

CLARE. I said, 'Let's get our names down pronto,' didn't I? 'That looks like a lovely thing to do.'

Josie Fowler had her name on the list as well but. Well, they Tippexed it out.

Pause.

MARION. They'll be nearly done in there, surely! No one at the desk! Anyone could walk in.

(*To* GRACE.) Now, I'm just going to park you here, okay?

ALF. A load of clueless teenagers traipsing through earlier –

MARION. Teenagers? / What were they doing?

ALF. Trousers hanging halfway down their backsides.

CLARE. For Josie. / Grandchildren probably.

ALF. Gawping at us, like they were on safari. They think we were born old.

SADIE. It's not their fault, you were the same when you were their age, how can you know? My granddaughter and her friends, they all think the world will wait for them, we were the same.

ALF. Head full of wire wool half of them. They've got nothing about them, I was never as gormless as the teenagers now.

SADIE. That's what you think. I was two years below you at Mannington Grammar, we all called you Alfie Two-Tries because you always tried it on twice.

ALF (*laughter*). That'll be right! Oh, dear me, that's made my day! Two-Tries! Yes, that was me. Oh, dear God.

MARION. Ooh, I know what I was going to ask you. How have you got on with those support tights I brought in last week?

CLARE. I haven't had a chance yet. They're in my bedside drawer still. I'm waiting for Barbara or someone to give me a hand with them.

ALF. I can give you a hand with them if you like. (*Laughs*.)

CLARE (*to* MARION). Just ignore him.

ALF (*to* SADIE). You were two years below me at Mannington, were you? Well, I say.

SADIE. You've already tried it on twice with me so don't waste your time.

ALF (*laughter*). Oh, that's made my day, that really has. Two-Tries Barratt, you're absolutely right. Well, stick that in your pipe and smoke it. You couldn't fit that in your memory box. Well I never.

CLARE. I think someone will be free to help me with the tights this week, they've been rushed off their feet with Josie Fowler passing away. It'll calm down now.

MARION. Until the next one.

CLARE. Marion!

MARION. Well.

CLARE. What a terrible thing to say.

MARION. Yes, sorry. I didn't think.

CLARE. Well, you should think. How would you like it, stuck in here –

MARION. It's hard for me too, I'm older than you!

CLARE. You're not stuck in here though, are you?

MARION. It's very stressful for me, on my own at the house, walking the dogs twice a day, keeping on top of it all. It's difficult. I'm just waiting to fall over and not be able to get up. On my own.

CLARE. Well, at least you can get around. I'm a hostage to my hip.

MARION. I know.

CLARE. My hip's never going to be the same as it was.

MARION. I know.

MARION *tries not to cry*.

CLARE. Come on now. Chin up.

MARION. Yes. I am.

CLARE. And Penny and Phil are around, aren't they, they'll pop in if you need anything, won't they?

MARION. They're away. The car hasn't been in the drive since Sunday night. I'm fine! I'm too busy to be lonely!

CLARE. It might be in the garage. It might need an MOT.

MARION. No, I'm pretty sure they're away, it's very quiet.

Pause.

I'm fine! I've got a hundred and thirty mobile-phone covers to run up on the machine for the school's tabletop sale. They rang me up! 'Miss Jessop,' they said, 'I hope you're not going to let us down!' / Too busy to feel sorry for myself!

CLARE. I don't know why you say yes to all these things!

MARION. I know! They raised nearly three hundred pounds on that stall last year, they said. 'We're relying on you!' I don't know how I ever had time to work, honestly, I can't fit it all in!

GRACE *starts to agitate in her chair.*

All right there, Grace?

GRACE. Is Josie in there? Is Josie in there with them?

CLARE. Josie's dead, Grace. She died last week, didn't she. That's why we can't go into the dining room.

GRACE. Is Harry there with her?

CLARE. Don't you remember, the end-of-life team came in, first thing Tuesday I think it was. A week last Tuesday.

(*To* MARION.) She's got no one. Not a single visitor, she's been here eighteen months, and no one's been in. Isn't it terrible?

MARION. Terrible.

(*To* GRACE.) Can I get anything for you, Grace? Would you like me to find the tea trolley?

CLARE. Do you want my sister to get you a cup of tea?

GRACE. No! I don't want tea.

CLARE. Okay. Well, that's all right.

GRACE. I want to see the baby.

CLARE. What baby?

GRACE. Harry's baby. My baby. I want to hold the baby!

CLARE (*to* MARION). The sense gets lost, you see. No one knows what anyone's talking about half the time.

MARION (*to* GRACE). There's no baby here. You'll be allowed back in the dining room soon, so all back to normal in no time, don't you worry, Grace.

(*To* CLARE *and* SADIE.) I'm doing their job now, it's like I work here! We're the lucky ones really. It's just a tiny bit of arthritis with me, I'm fine apart from that, still got my mind, lucky really.

SADIE. We are lucky really.

MARION. This is ridiculous! I'm going to see what's going on.

MARION *exits*.

EDDIE *starts singing soulfully. He has a lovely voice*.

EDDIE (*singing*). It's a grand old team to play for,
It's a grand old team to support,
And if you know your history,
It's enough to make your heart go ooo,
We don't care what the red side say,
What the heck do we care,
Cos we only know there's going to be a show,
When the Everton boys are there.

SADIE. My granddaughter says to me, 'The world's different now, Gran, it's not like when you were young, it's all changed.' She says I'm better off not having to deal with things, I get so confused, you see. She says, 'You're better off in Sea View, Gran, they can cater to your needs in there.' But what she can't understand is, I still feel the same, the world might have changed, you might have your cappuccinos and your internet shopping and what have you, but has it really changed that much? We're all still people, aren't we? I still feel like I did when I was sixteen. Stepping off the bus in my new skirt and heels, feeling like a proper lady on my way in to my first day at work. No more school! I remember it like it was just the other day. The first time I saw my Ray, with his collar up and his dad's smart coat, waiting for me on the corner so he could pretend he was just passing, oh, the butterflies in my stomach as I walked towards him! I thought my legs would give way beneath me.

ALF. Old Alfie Two-Tries! That's very good. That's tickled me that has.

SADIE. My granddaughter's moving to York in the new year, got a teaching post at the university there. She got a first-class degree, you see.

MARION *re-enters with a tea towel, drying a cup.*

MARION. Right, ladies and gentlemen, all clear now.

The urn's on. Now who wants what?

ALF. All clear now, is it?

MARION. Yes. Barbara's just taking Mrs Webster back to her room for a lie-down. She said, 'If you want to use the dining room it's all yours.'

ALF. All the stragglers gone now, have they?

MARION. Yes, all gone. I said to Barbara, 'It's like I work here! I'm doing your job now!' She said, 'Oh, lovely, thanks ever so much, we could do with an extra pair of hands!'

SADIE. A good send-off, was it? Did Barbara say?

MARION. She didn't say. I expect so though.

SADIE. I should have gone in. I didn't feel up to it really.

MARION. There's half a tray of sandwiches left in there! I said to Barbara, 'I'll nab these, shall I?' She said, 'Go ahead, why not?' Salmon, some of them.

SADIE. I say my goodbyes in my own way.

God rest her soul.

MARION. The tea trolley's in there, we're just waiting for the urn. So it's all back to normal. Business as usual! Everyone all right?

ALL (*except* GRACE *and* EDDIE). Yes.

MARION. You all right, Mr, umm – ?

CLARE / SADIE. Pope.

MARION. You all right there, Mr Pope?

EDDIE. And of course, Morpeth, Egerton, Wallasey, Alfred, Great Float, Vittoria and Bidston Docks they were on the opposite bank, you see. All gone now.

MARION. Yes, that's such a shame, isn't it?

EDDIE looks at MARION, *he meets her eye.*

EDDIE. It is a shame. It breaks your heart.

MARION. Yes.

Pause.

And Grace, okay, is she?

MARION *goes over to* GRACE *and takes her hand.*

Would you like me to bring you a nice cup of tea, Grace, in your special cup?

GRACE. Josie?

MARION. No, love. It's Miss Jessop's sister. I'm going to bring you a nice cup of tea, okay?

GRACE. I want to talk to Josie. I'm ready to talk to Josie now.

MARION *looks at* CLARE *and* SADIE, *a bit panicked.*

CLARE. It's okay, Grace.

SADIE. There we are, now. Yes.

MARION. That's good.

MARION *stays and strokes her hand for a while. Then she gets up and goes to the door.*

Let's see about this urn.

ALF. Hey, Miss Jessop's sister! How about you and me? Where do you fancy going? A club? A slap-up meal?

MARION. Oh, well! I don't know!

ALF. Come on, it's on me, I'll treat you, get your glad rags on, let's hit the town!

MARION. Oh no, I'm at my choir practice tonight.

ALF. They won't miss you just this once, will they? It's two for one up the Legion tonight!

MARION. Don't tempt me!

ALF *and* MARION *laugh.*

Lights fade.

Scene Three

Two weeks earlier. In JOSIE's *room in the home.*

JOSIE *lies in bed, very still.*

EMMA *sits on a chair doing some homework on her laptop.* FAY *sits on the floor looking at her phone.*

In the corner of the room stands a young man in 1950s army uniform, JOSIE's *husband* HARRY. EMMA *and* FAY *don't see him or hear him. The only lines they can hear are* <u>underlined</u>.

Silence apart from a clock ticking and the occasional sounds from the corridor outside.

HARRY (*softly*). Josie.

Josephine.

HARRY *moves to the edge of the bed.*

Josie.

HARRY *gently sits on the edge of the bed. He takes out a packet of cigarettes and a lighter, he goes to light up.*

JOSIE. You can't smoke in here.

HARRY. Who says?

JOSIE. Put them away, you can't smoke in here.

HARRY. Why not?

JOSIE. You can't smoke in hospital, there's signs all over.

HARRY. We're not in a hospital, this a hospital?

JOSIE. Isn't it? I thought it was. I don't know.

> JOSIE *sits up a bit.*

> What are you wearing that for?

HARRY. What?

JOSIE. That get-up. / Your uniform!

HARRY. It's my uniform. / What's up with it?

> *Pause.*

JOSIE. <u>Oh, Harry.</u> It's good to see you again.

> EMMA *and* FAY *look up.*

EMMA. Are you all right, Nanny?

> *Silence.*

FAY. Did she say Harry?

EMMA. I think so.

> (*To* JOSIE.) It's me and Fay, Nanny. Harry's at tae kwon do. Mum's gone to pick him up.

> *Silence.*

FAY. Shall I text Mum? See where they are.

EMMA. No, she'll be here in a minute.

> EMMA *and* FAY *go back to what they were doing.*

> *After a moment.*

HARRY. I walked round the back way, the long way round. I wanted to see if the daffs were out in the field at the top. The sun was coming up, the light was bouncing off the yellow, I wanted to climb up onto the stone wall and shout your name at the top of my voice.

JOSIE. You better not have done.

HARRY. I wanted to.

JOSIE. You didn't, did you? / Making an exhibition of yourself.

HARRY. I don't care who hears me.

JOSIE. Scaring everyone awake with your nonsense.

HARRY. Are you going to come with me now, Josie?

JOSIE. I don't know if I'm coming or going.

HARRY. You're coming *and* going. It pulls you all ways.

JOSIE. Ever such a funny feeling.

HARRY. Go with it, I've got you.

Pause.

JOSIE. I don't know which is the top and which is the bottom. There's splinters of me scattered all over the place. Am I in bed, Harry?

HARRY. Yes and no.

JOSIE. What kind of an answer is that? You're no help.

HARRY (*softly*). Josie.

JOSIE. Yes.

HARRY (*softly*). Josie.

JOSIE. What?

HARRY. Come on, girl. It's getting late. Let's go.

Pause.

EMMA *stands and stretches her legs.*

FAY. Where are you going?

EMMA. Nowhere. My leg's gone to sleep.

FAY. Liam keeps texting me to see if I'm going to Billy's.

EMMA. Have you texted back?

FAY. Do you think I should?

EMMA. If you want to. Have you got those crisps Mum gave us?

FAY *hands* EMMA *a packet of crisps.*

EMMA *goes over to* JOSIE*, smoothes her sheet. Kisses her face.*

Love you, Nanny.

EMMA *sits back down and carries on with her work.*

HARRY *watches* EMMA *and* FAY *for a moment, then looks back to* JOSIE.

HARRY (*softly*). Josie.

JOSIE *sits up in bed.*

JOSIE. Did we make a mess of things, Harry?

HARRY. We did well. We made the best of it.

JOSIE. We tried our best, didn't we? Tried to get it right.

HARRY. We did.

JOSIE. I worry about Andrew. He's never found his way.

HARRY. You took him into your heart like he was your own. You brought him up like he was your own flesh and blood, there's not many women who would have done what you did.

JOSIE. My mother said I should leave you. Pack a bag, take Melanie, up and off. I could have gone full time at Wickhams, you know, they said I could. My mother would have had Mel.

HARRY. She never liked me.

JOSIE. No, and she liked you even less when you went with that slapper.

HARRY. We're going to rake over all this now, are we?

I just said, there's not many women would've done what you did, I know what it took you.

JOSIE. It was so humiliating, the way they all looked at me.

HARRY. I just said, didn't I?

JOSIE. Gracie's brothers all giving us daggers every time we stepped foot out the house. Like I'd stolen something that was theirs. I wanted to say, 'She would've killed this baby if it was up to her. I've saved a life, not taken one, so you can stop with the evil stares.'

HARRY. It's all in the past now, Josie. What good does it do to dig it all up?

JOSIE. And she couldn't have looked after him! Couldn't look after a sock in a box that one. Useless she was. All that rouge she used to slather on, what were you thinking!

HARRY. I wasn't myself. I'd lost my mother, I was chucked out the army, wasn't I? I had lost sight of it all.

Pause.

YOUNG HARRY *enters the room tentatively.*

YOUNG HARRY. Hi.

EMMA. Hi.

YOUNG HARRY. Mum's talking to someone in the office. Have you got my crisps?

FAY hands him his crisps.

EMMA. Nanny said your name.

YOUNG HARRY. Did she?

FAY. Oh yeah.

YOUNG HARRY. What did she say?

EMMA. Just Harry, 'Oh, Harry.'

YOUNG HARRY. What else?

EMMA. Nothing.

YOUNG HARRY. Cool.

YOUNG HARRY *goes to her. He stands awkwardly beside the bed for a while.*

Hi, Nanna. I'm here. I'm back from tae kwon do.

Pause.

It was good.

YOUNG HARRY *goes and sits on the windowsill and eats his crisps.* EMMA *and* FAY *go back to what they were doing.*

EMMA. Did you text Liam?

FAY. Yeah. I just said 'dunno'.

EMMA. Has he texted back?

FAY. Not yet, no.

YOUNG HARRY. Keep us posted.

JOSIE. Who's talking? Is that my voice, Harry?

HARRY. You're shouting the place down.

JOSIE. It's me doing all that talking, is it?

HARRY. I've got you.

JOSIE. <u>Is it Andrew? I want Andrew.</u>

YOUNG HARRY *looks up.*

YOUNG HARRY. Did you hear that? She wants Uncle Andrew.

FAY. Oh my God, get Mum.

Is Uncle Andrew here?

EMMA. I don't think he's coming till the weekend. (*To* JOSIE.) Uncle Andrew's coming at the weekend, Nanny.

HARRY *takes her hand.*

JOSIE. Get off me, what are you doing here anyway?

HARRY. Sitting with you, aren't I.

JOSIE. I don't know if I'm coming or going.

HARRY. Hold my hand then.

JOSIE. I can't hold your hand, I don't know where my hand is, I've gone small, I can't get myself back in the right places.

<u>Where's Andrew?</u>

EMMA. He's coming at the weekend, Nanny.

(*To* YOUNG HARRY.) Get Mum.

HARRY *sings, softly, the first few lines of 'My Girl Josephine' by Fats Domino.*

JOSIE. <u>Give over, I'm not in the mood for singing.</u>

EMMA (*laughs*). You don't have to sing, Nanny!

FAY. Maybe she wants us to sing, do you think?

YOUNG HARRY. Sing what?

FAY *sings the first line of 'My Girl Josephine'.*

EMMA. Go and get Mum, Harry. Those crisps stink.

YOUNG HARRY *exits the room.*

FAY *and* EMMA *sing the next two lines of the song together.*

And then, for one moment, the two worlds synchronise and HARRY, FAY *and* EMMA *sing the fourth line of the song together.*

FAY. Oh my God, my voice is so rubbish!

EMMA. I bet Harry tries to get Mum to buy him a drink from that machine by the lifts.

FAY. I can't tell if she likes it or not. She's probably like, 'Shut up!'

FAY *checks her phone.* EMMA *arranges things on the bedside table. Reads a card.*

HARRY *sits on the edge of the bed.*

HARRY *sings the next three lines of the song.*

JOSIE. What are you doing here, you fool.

HARRY. Singing to you, aren't I, like I used to do.

JOSIE. Give over.

EMMA. Mel's coming, Nanny. (*To* FAY.) She knows we're here.

FAY. Do you want us to sing to you, Nanny? Harry's gone to get Mum. Mum's coming.

EMMA. Mel's coming, Nanny. It's okay.

FAY. Shall we keep singing to her?

EMMA. No. Wait till Mum gets here.

EMMA and FAY *hover at the foot of the bed.*

HARRY *takes* JOSIE*'s hand, she lets him.*

The clock in the room is ticking louder than usual.

HARRY. Come on, Josie, that's right.

Pause.

I've got you.

Pause.

Let me walk you home.

JOSIE *looks at* HARRY *as –*

Lights fade.

The End.